THE MYSTERY OF THE INCARNATION

THE
MYSTERY
OF THE
INCARNATION

CARDINAL CHRISTOPH SCHÖNBORN

Translated by Graham Harrison

Paulist Press
New York / Mahwah, NJ

Cover image courtesy of Shutterstock
Cover and book design by Lynn Else

Original published as DAS GEHEIMNIS DER MENSCHWERDUNG
(1983)

Copyright © 1992 by Johannes Verlag Einsiedeln, Freiburg:
WEIHNACHT - MYTHOS WIRD WIRKLICHKEIT

First English language edition published in 1992 by Ignatius Press

Library of Congress Cataloging-in-Publication Data

Schönborn, Christoph von.
    [Weihnacht, Mythos wird Wirklichkeit. English.]
    The mystery of the Incarnation / Cardinal Christoph Schönborn.
        pages cm
    Includes bibliographical references.
    ISBN 978-0-8091-4851-6 (alk. paper) — ISBN 978-1-58768-361-9
    1. Incarnation—Meditations. I. Title.
    BT220.S3813 2013
    232`.1—dc23

                                                        2013025518

ISBN: 978-0-8091-4851-6 (paperback)
ISBN 978-1-58768-361-9 (e-book)

Published by Paulist Press in 2013 by special arrangement with
Johannes Verlag Einsiedeln
997 Macarthur Boulevard
Mahwah, New Jersey 07430

www.paulistpress.com

Printed and bound in the
United States of America

Contents

Introduction

In spite of all the commercialism and hectic activity associated with it, Christmas continues to fascinate so many people in a way the other festivals of the Church do not. It even fascinates those who hold aloof from the Church's faith. Why is this? It is not merely a harking-back to the dreams of childhood, a tendency reinforced by the trials of adult life. Might not the reverse be the case? Perhaps Christmas fascinates us because all of us *know deep down*, in some way or other, that the birth of this Child has something to do with the deepest longings and hopes that, even today, we still have not managed to shake off.

The tinsel side of Christmas, after all, is only trying to divert some of this longing into the channels of Yuletide commerce. It is a borrowed radiance and its success doesn't only demonstrate indirectly the strength of the *longing* for the advent of the New Man, the Redeemer; it shows that the Christmas radiance is itself a reflection of that Light, which has shone forth in the Incarnation of God.

The following four theological meditations are an attempt to present something of this fundamental radiance. First comes a preliminary account of the mythical elements in our faith, and then we follow the three sections of our

Creed: "He came down from heaven;" "He was incarnate of the Virgin Mary through the Holy Spirit;" and "He became man." The final meditation on the Christmas icon is perhaps the most important part, for it often happens that the mystery's radiance shines forth in the work of the artist with more impact than in the theologian's discourse. Accordingly, the reader is at liberty to start with this final chapter.

"Myth Became Fact"

Can a rational human being be expected to believe that a God, or a Son of God, "came down from heaven," "took flesh," was born of a virgin, and, after the dramatic conclusion of his earthly career, "ascended into heaven" again? Are we not at the heart of myth here? Can we expect people today to regard such mythological assertions as truth?

In England in 1977, seven noted theologians wrote a book with the deliberately provocative title *The Myth of God Incarnate*. In its preface, the authors unmistakably and honestly set forth their conviction that Christian teaching today needs a clear change of direction:

> The need arises from growing knowledge of Christian origins, and involves a recognition that Jesus was (as he is presented in Acts 2:21) "a man approved by God" for a special role within the divine purpose, and that the later conception of him as God incarnate, the Second Person of the Holy Trinity living a human life, is a mythological or poetic way of expressing his significance for us. This recognition is called for in the interests of truth… (Hick, ix)

The change of course here called for is a radical one. Jesus is a man approved by God; incarnation is a mythical mode of speech designed to tell *us* that Jesus is important. This implies that the notion of the Divine Trinity is on shaky ground, as is the question of Jesus' divinity. Not that all such talk is simply false; it is true in the way a myth is true; in other words, as imagery, as a symbolic and poetic way of expressing that something has very special significance. Not surprisingly, the book by these seven authors unleashed a veritable storm of debate. We shall try to use this debate as the starting-point for our own observations, since it raises a number of essential preliminary questions connected with our topic.

INCARNATION AND MYTH

Christian faith speaks about the Son of God who, in order to become incarnate, comes down from heaven and returns thither after having accomplished what he was sent to do. There are *similarities* between this and the myths of other religions, which speak of gods who descend to earth, die, and are subsequently resurrected. There is nothing new about this. Even early Christian authors make reference to parallels of this kind; at the most they are regarded as a kind of premonition of the revelation that was to take place in Christ, but in the main they are treated as a mere plagiarization of the Christian teaching. Since the nineteenth century, the historico-critical method generally takes the opposite direction. It does not explain the myths as plagiarization of the biblical revelation; rather—vice versa—it sees the language of the Bible and particularly of the New Testament as the result of the influence of particular extra-biblical myths.

The so-called "history of religions" school interpreted the ancient mystery-cults as the "matrix" of the Christian myth. In the ceremonies of initiation into the Eleusinian mysteries; in the sharing in the death, burial, and resurrection of Osiris; in the rebirth of the votaries of Cybele who, using bull's blood, achieved union with the dead and resurrected god; scholars thought they had found the "spiritual climate" that could have given rise to the Christian myth of the incarnation, death, and resurrection of the heavenly Son of God, and the associated Christian rite whereby the believer dies with Christ and rises with him (Rahner, 19–54). It was as a result of the work of R. Bultmann that the theory of myth proposed by the "history of religions" school attained wide currency, for he related it to his program of "demythologization." Thus, the theory became one element of an all-embracing revision of the Christian proclamation and of Christianity's understanding of itself. As a result, the problems associated with "myth" emerged from the confines of a purely historical discussion (the whole question of sources) and constituted a fundamental issue: What is the function of mythical speech?

An *historical* critique was applied at a very early date to the origins of the Christian belief in the Incarnation. Today it is appropriate to re-examine this critique, since it has become almost fashionable again to trace all manner of elements in Christianity back to possible (and frankly impossible) parallels in other religions. No less a scholar than Adolf von Harnack energetically opposed this confusing of sources, "that comparative mythology which tries to find a causal connection between everything, tearing down firm boundaries, lightheartedly ignoring the chasms which separate whole areas and often dreaming up links on the basis of the most superficial similarities" needs to be overcome. He goes on: "By this means people can in a trice make Christ into a sun-god and the twelve apostles into the twelve months; the story of the birth of Christ reminds them of all the other stories of divine births; the dove at Christ's baptism prompts them to recall all the doves in mythology, and the donkey in Christ's triumphal entry into Jerusalem just *has* to be linked with all the other famous donkeys. Thus, using the wand of the 'history of religions' school, they succeed in eliminating every spontaneous trait" (Rahner, 25ff.).

Particularly as regards the doctrine of the Incarnation of the Son of God, careful historical examination of the sources has shown with increasing clarity that it cannot be put down to the influence of some (vague) Iranian redeemer-myth (R. Bultmann) or of Hellenistic mystery cults. The images and concepts of the primitive Church's faith in the Incarnation belong first and foremost to the world of Old Testament faith (Hengel, 1974).

This, however, does not give us an answer to the question of myth itself. True, nowadays we see more clearly that the picture of Christ we find in Paul and in the primitive Church is, in general, largely shaped by Jewish ideas. But the stark question remains: are not these after all *mythical* ideas, whether of Hellenistic or of Jewish origin?

The *genetic* question leads to the question of *fact*; the question of *historical origin* leads to the question of *truth*. The issue is not simply whether notions of God's Incarnation originated, historically speaking, in myth, but primarily whether mythical notions are true, and if so, how. *This* is the nub of the whole debate. The seven English authors are also concerned about the *question of truth* when they describe the Incarnation as *myth*. John Hick, one of the seven, defines myth as follows:

"A myth is a story, which is told, but is not literally true, or an idea or an image which is applied to a person or a thing, but is not literally true, but induces a certain attitude or opinion in the listener." (Hick, p. 188)

At a first reading, the question of truth is given a clear answer here: the Incarnation is a myth; that is, it is *not literally true*. Rather it is pictorial, metaphorical, poetic, symbolic language. Is this opposition between "literally true" and "pictorial and metaphorical" tenable? Let us explore this question in connection with the article of the creed: "He came down from heaven."

MYTH AND REALITY

The period following the Second Vatican Council—not always very inspiring—saw many liturgical experiments. On one occasion, an Old Testament scholar who had a keen interest in liturgy attempted to make a translation of the Psalms for liturgical use from which he had expunged all the images that, allegedly, were alien to "modern man." There was no longer a deer yearning for the running streams; the Lord no longer had a rod and staff to give me comfort; and the longing "to dwell in the house of the Lord all the days of my life" was turned into the pale privilege of "being always near to God." Why had the Psalms' strong poetic images been replaced by pale, banal ones?

It is a mistake to think that we can speak *without* using images and metaphors. Even scientific language is full of metaphors. Does this mean that everything we say by means of metaphors is "not literally true?" If I say, "the audience hung spellbound on his lips," no one imagines that they *lit-*

erally hung on his lips. On the other hand, no one would conclude that the expression is purely subjective and does not refer to an objective reality: the audience is *really* fascinated and listens "as if spellbound." The metaphor "hanging on someone's lips" is meant to underline precisely the *reality* of the audience's involvement.

However, the seven English authors think that "literally true" language refers to objective facts, whereas mythic, metaphorical, and figurative language is the expression of subjective attitudes and feelings. This is an untenable assumption. Image and myth also refer to reality, and not merely to subjective attitudes and feelings. But they refer to reality in a *different way* from the "literal" language; that is, through images.

Today we are continually being faced with this either/or: Is the statement, "Jesus is the incarnate Son of God" to be taken *literally* or in a symbolic, mythical sense? Was Jesus born of the *Virgin* Mary in a *literal* or *metaphorical* sense? The answer of the seven Englishmen is clear:

> "That Jesus was God the Son incarnate is not literally true, *since it has no literal meaning*, but it is an application to Jesus of a mythical concept...; it offers a way of declaring his significance to the world." (Hick, 178; italics added)

To find a way out of this cul-de-sac, I would like to refer to another English author who has thought about myth more than most of our contemporaries, himself a writer of wonderful myths, and whose path brought him—in a unique way—via myths to faith: C. S. Lewis (1898–1963).

When he was a young lecturer at Oxford, C. S. Lewis,

like many of his (and our) educated contemporaries, sub-scribed to the view that Christianity was simply a re-casting of old myths. Like Sigmund Freud, Lewis had read J. G. Frazer's monumental twelve-volume work, *The Golden Bough* (1890–1915), and was fascinated by the plethora of parallels, drawn from the history of religions, to the idea of the "dying god."

> The myths of Adonis and Osiris, who are killed only to rise again, so renewing the life of nature and of their votaries, are nothing other than myths of natural growth, symbolically applying a natural process to human life. Every year the corn dies, is laid in the earth as seed, and subsequently rises up to a new and more abundant life; so man too has to go through death in order to attain life. The young Lewis was of the opin-ion that the stories of Jesus were simply another myth of natural growth. Jesus says that the grain of wheat must die if it is to bear fruit; he takes bread, i.e., grain, in his hands, breaks it and says, 'This is my body'; he dies the following day and rises from the dead three days later: is not this Jesus simply another harvest-god, a corn-king, giving his life for the life of the world? One evening, however, Lewis heard another commit-ted atheist remark during a conversation that the evi-dence for the historicity of the Gospels was surprisingly good: 'A strange thing: all that stuff of Frazer's about the dying God—it almost looks as though it actually happened once.' (Kranz, 71; Brague)

In his autobiography, *Surprised by Joy*, Lewis says that this conversation was a decisive step on his path to conversion. From childhood Lewis had been fascinated by myths. What was it in them that so strangely moved him? It is that they awaken in the reader a longing for something that is beyond his grasp. Myths have this fascination because they effect a *catharsis*, that is, they shake us up and purify us; thus, they expand our consciousness, allowing us through them to transcend ourselves. So myths are not "poets' deceptions" (as Plato said in his *Republic*), nor demonic delusions (as many of the Church Fathers thought), nor clerical lies (as many Enlightenment figures asserted); rather "Myth in general is…at its best, a real though unfocused gleam of divine truth falling on human imagination" (Lewis, *Miracles*, 134).

Surely, the reason why the great myths of the nations have something in common with the story of the Son of God who came down from heaven for our sake is that there is a trace, in the imagination of great pagan teachers and myth-makers, of that very Incarnation that, according to our faith, is the core of all cosmic history.

The distinction between myth and Christian history is not simply that between false and true; myths are not false simply because they are myths. C. S. Lewis sees the relationship between myth and Christian history as the difference "between a *real* event on the one hand and blurred dreams and intimations of this same event on the other hand."

The heart of Christianity is a myth which is also a fact. The old myth of the Dying God, *without ceasing to be myth*, comes down from the heaven of legend and imagination to the earth of history. It *happens* at a particular date, in a particular place, followed by definable historical consequences. We pass from a Balder or an Osiris, dying nobody knows when or where, to a historical

Person crucified *under Pontius Pilate*. By becoming fact it does not cease to be myth: that is the miracle. (Lewis, *God in the Dock*, 66–67)

C. S. Lewis encourages us not to be afraid if we find that Christianity has parallels to myth. Would it not be a pity if Christianity, in order to assert its truth, had to reject all prior intimations of this truth? If Christianity is to fulfill the "longings of the nations," it does not need to reject the expression of this longing as it is found in the myths. It sounds like a theological manifesto when Lewis says, "*We do not need to be ashamed of the mythical luminosity which attaches to our theology.*" All creative theology lives and draws sustenance from this "mythical luminosity," which our theology still bears. "Demythologization," conceived as the task of a "theology for today," misses the fact that the "secularization" of our world is only one side: on the other side there is a flourishing world of myths—although seen in different garb, for example, the world of science fiction. Here, as in former times, we find the great themes of mythology: monsters and demons, gods and spirits.

Johann Georg Hamann once said, "Unless our theology is worth as much as mythology, it will be simply impossible for us to reach the level of pagan poetry, let alone surpass it." It is not a question of setting myth against reality; because of a defective understanding of "reality," doing so leads inevitably to the repression of the symbolic dimension of the Christian message, what one might call its "mythical luminosity." But it is equally mistaken to reduce the historical reality of the events of Incarnation, Cross, and Resurrection to a "merely" symbolic significance, as Gnosticism did. Rather we must say that the history of

Christ is the "highest myth" because, in it, myth has become reality (Lewis, *God in the Dock*).

WHAT IF IT WERE SO?

This is the direction we shall take in what follows, as we ask: What is the meaning of God's Incarnation? We shall try to show that the power of symbolism of such images as "came down from heaven," "born of the Virgin Mary," "and was made man," lies precisely in the fact that here symbol and reality, myth and life, coincide. However, before we set out on this path we must go into one final preliminary question.

In *The Myth of God Incarnate,* we read the following sentence: "That Jesus was God the Son incarnate is not literally true, *since it has no literal meaning*" (Hick, 175; italics added). This view is supported by further remarks by the various authors.

1. "Humanity cannot, without ceasing to be humanity, be the expression, embodiment, contingent form of God" (Goulder, 63). Put more simply, this means that it is impossible for God to become *man*, because a God who did so would not be a genuine man.
2. "When we move over to speaking of God *being* part of his own creation or a part of that creation *being* God, *Prima facie* this does seem to me to involve logical self-contradiction" (Goulder, 6). In other words, the Incarnation of God—God becoming a creature—contradicts God's being *as God*.

No doubt it would be necessary to examine these two statements in more detail and set forth their implications in a more nuanced way. All the same, it is quite clear from the context that, as far as these seven authors are concerned, the idea of *real* Incarnation of God is just as absurd as a "square circle." Their idea of man and their idea of God are equally incompatible with the notion of a real Incarnation. Here we have come up against a limit that cannot be passed by adducing more arguments. If the above principles are taken as fundamental, what Christians say about "the Son of God coming down" *can* only be understood as a myth in the sense of something that is "not literally true."

In this situation, we can only ask—not in a triumphalist manner, but by way of an invitation—"But what if, all the same, it *were* so…?" What if the substance expressed in so many myths like the echo of a great yearning, a shadowy presentiment, has actually become reality?

He Came Down from Heaven

"O that thou wouldst rend the heavens and come down, that the mountains might quake at thy presence…to make thy name known to thy adversaries, and that the nations might tremble at thy presence. When thou didst terrible things which we looked not for, thou camest down, the mountains quaked at thy presence. From of old no one has heard…." (Isa 64:1–4)

The anonymous sixth-century prophet who produced this cry of hope and longing calls for the coming of God. In doing so, he refers to an event that, for Israel, is unforgettable: the exodus from Egypt. In its deliverance from bondage in Egypt, Israel sees the prototype of all redemption. Did not God then *come down* in order to save his people? In the vision of the Burning Bush, God speaks to Moses: "I have seen the affliction of my people who are in Egypt, and have heard their cry because of their taskmasters; I know their sufferings, and I *have come down* to deliver them out of the hand of the Egyptians, and to *bring them up* out of that land to a good and broad land, a land flowing with milk and honey" (Exod 3:7–8).

The "fundamental experience" of deliverance from Egypt gave Israel the certainty and an ever-new hope that God is not afraid to *come down* into the midst of his people in order to *lead it up* to the Promised Land. We find in the Prophets images of astounding intimacy: "The Lord, your God, is in your midst, a warrior who gives victory; he will rejoice over you with gladness, he will renew you in his love; he will exult over you with loud singing as on a day of festival" (Zeph 3:17). Later Jewish theology never ceases to be amazed at this descent of God. So we read in the commentary on Exodus 13:21 ("And the Lord went before them…by night in a pillar of fire to give them light"), "R. Jose the Galilean said: If it were not written in Scripture it would be forbidden to say such things, that a father carries a torch before his children, a master before his slave" (Kuhn, 23). God, whose transcendence is such a marked feature of the faith of Israel, is also the One who is very near: he comes down, makes himself small, adopts human proportions. In Jewish theology, this dwelling of God among his people is called the *shekinah*: his "indwelling," his "glorious nearness." The *shekinah* is both distinct from God and yet himself. And it is emphasized "that God's dwelling (in his people) was the ultimate goal of the divine plan of creation, a goal envisaged right at the beginning of creation" (Kuhn, 64). God is seen entirely in the context of his dwelling among men: He "*is* entirely his dwelling among men" (Kuhn, 69).

The Christian faith in God's Incarnation is in line with his Old Testament Jewish hope and expectation:

"God has come down from heaven to his people out of love; he has chosen the humblest place on earth and limited his affinity to a small space in the world; poor and humble, he renounced the honor due to him, performed the work of a slave for mankind's sake; and finally, in a concrete way, he shared in the deepest pain of his people. Not only can the Jewish faith affirm this: it is also the basis of the Christian profession of faith." (Kuhn, 105)

True, there remains one fundamental difference: in Judaism, necessarily, there is always a reluctance

"to associate God, as the One Person that He is in Judaism, *fully and finally with a human life*, since this would seem to put God's transcendence in jeopardy. God can adopt particular features of an earthly existence, but he can never really 'become flesh' in a final and irrevocable way and so 'dwell among us' (John 1:14). Accordingly he could not experience the ultimate gravity of such a human life, i.e., death." (Kuhn, 108)

So we find the rabbis explicitly rejecting the ultimate consequence of God's "descent"; for example, Rabbi Jose: "God never really came down upon the earth," for, however small the distance between them, God and man can never quite come together (Kuhn, 72).

According to the same Rabbi Jose, God always stays ten hand's breadths above the earth; that is, "God has never come to earth completely, nor have men ascended to him completely" (Kuhn, 45ff.). Thus we could rightly say that the Old Testament picture of God was characterized by an "*inclination* on God's part toward Incarnation" (Mauser, 16). Yet this inclination "hovers" in a kind of indecision. There continue to be new experiences of God's nearness, but also of his withdrawal and turning-away from man, and so the hope is always rekindled that, in the end, God will dwell among men permanently. A time will come when "my dwelling place shall be with them; and I will be their God, and they shall be my people" (Ezek 37:27; cf. Rev 21:3). This final and definitive dwelling of God among men remains the great promise of the Old Testament.

It is the faith of Christians that God has finally pitched his tent among men. Christians find this ultimate coming promised in countless passages of the Old Testament, and they see it fulfilled in the apparently insignificant birth of Jesus.

Born of the Virgin Mary

> "God on earth, God among men, not in the fire and to the accompaniment of trumpets, not on the smoking mountain…giving laws, but communing in bodily form, gently and kindly, with those like himself. God in flesh…so that, related to us by his flesh, he can lead all mankind back to God."

Here Basil the Great, in his Christmas homily, celebrates the fulfillment of the Old Testament promise in the physical birth of Christ. Again (Exod 3:8), we find the theme of God's coming down in order to lead his people up to him. What is new, however, is that the one who thus descends "to lead mankind back to God" is the *Son of God*, the Father's eternal Word: "The Word was made flesh and has pitched his tent among us" (John 1:14). The Son, "sent by God when the fullness of time had come" (Gal 4:4), is himself, according to Christian belief, "God from God, Light from Light, True God from True God." Thus, the Christmas *kontakion* of Romanus the Melodist actually says, "a little child is the eternal God" (Gamber).

At this point, we may become a little uneasy. Dreams are often lovelier if they *remain* dreams. Perhaps the rich image-world of mythical ideas concerning God's coming down among men is attractive precisely because it is a world of images? Can we accept that the obscure birth of an unknown Galilean *is actually* what these images refer to? "A little child is the eternal God?" It is no surprise that reason continually refuses to give its consent here. And then to go on to assert that this Child is begotten by the Holy Spirit and born of a virgin, Mary: would it not be all much more beautiful and more meaningful if we took it as a metaphor? Taking it as *reality* is so difficult, so embarrassing and alien to modern sensibilities.

Karl Barth once remarked about the dogma of the Virgin Birth: "The Church knew what she was doing when she placed this dogma like a guard, as it were, at the entrance to the mystery of Christmas" (Barth, 198). In what follows, we shall look at the mystery of Christ's birth from the Virgin Mary as this kind of a "guard" placed at the door of the Incarnation. The realism of *both* mysteries will emerge as the necessary presupposition if both are to unfold the fullness of symbolic meaning they contain. First of all, therefore, we must approach the *historical* question, so that we can then go on to deal with the theological symbolism of the phrase "born of the Virgin Mary."

A HISTORICAL QUESTION, BUT MORE...

The conception of a human being is something very intimate. A mother will not speak of it in the same way as she tells of other events in the lives of her children. If and when she eventually does tell her son or daughter about it, she will do so with great care and modesty. The conception of Jesus by the Holy Spirit is not something that can be exposed to public curiosity like any marketplace novelty. In attempting to speak of it, we must adapt our speech to the intimacy and hiddenness of this event. At the same time, we must take care lest our faith and our reason fail to see the forest for the profusion of exegetical trees.

If the conception of Jesus by the Spirit is a concrete miracle, there are only two ways of knowing it: either Mary herself spoke about it or it was communicated to others by some kind of revelation. Alternatively, it is not a historical event at all, but a theological construct intended to express the special significance of Jesus.

Doubtless the historical question is a difficult one. Only Matthew and Luke speak of the Virgin Birth. Paul never mentions it, nor does Mark. It is disputed whether John was acquainted with it. At the same time, it is nowhere explicitly denied. Thus, the arguments for and against are largely based on the different interpretations of this silence (Vögtle, McHugh). The argument from silence must be handled with great caution.

The Church's post-apostolic tradition, however, is anything but silent. The second century is full of testimonies to the Virgin Birth. There can be no doubt that the second century Church was convinced of the *reality* of the virginal conception (except those parts of the Church that strayed into Gnosticism or other "heresies"). Here we can only cite the most essential witnesses. In the Old Roman Creed, which every candidate for baptism has to say, we find "...*natus est de Spiritu sancto ex Maria Virgine*—born of the Holy Spirit from the Virgin Mary": this is one of the fundamental elements of faith in Christ, beside Jesus' death and resurrection (Rordorf). "It is dear that no new and alien teaching could be introduced into a creed of this kind" (Machen, 4). If this is true of the second half of the second century, the testimony of the martyr bishop, Ignatius of Antioch, takes us back to the turn of the first-second centuries. Here, too, Christ's miraculous birth is one of the essential components of the profession of faith. Ignatius regards it as one of the "three eloquent mysteries which were wrought in the stillness of God," namely, "the virginity of Mary, her giving birth, and the death of the Lord" (Eph 19:1). For Ignatius, "our Lord...is in truth of the family of David according to the flesh, God's son by the will and power of God" (cf. Rom 1:3), "truly born of a Virgin...truly nailed to a tree in the flesh for our sakes under Pontius Pilate and Herod the Tetrarch..." (*Smyrn.* 1:1–2). Ignatius, writing in about AD 110, shows that as far as Antioch, his home, is concerned, as well as the Churches to which he is writing (Asia Minor, Rome), belief in the virginal conception of Jesus does not have to assert itself: it is part of the apostolic deposit of faith. This "article of faith" is also one of the clearest signs that Jesus was *really* man. It is striking that throughout the whole of the second century the Virgin Birth is never adduced as an argument for Jesus' *divinity*, but always for his true *humanity* (Machen, 7ff.; Edwards, 189–96; Gese, 46).

Where does the second century Church get her belief in this "eloquent mystery," Mary's virginity? Anyone who puts forward the view that the primitive Church invented this *theologoumenon* (i.e., opinion rather than doctrine) in order to underline the significance of Jesus must also be able to explain why the Church thus invented something that only gave her Jewish and pagan neighbors an occasion for mockery. It is illuminating to see the non-Christian reactions to the teaching on the Virgin Birth. Again, we can only give the briefest indications here.

In AD 155, the Christian philosopher-martyr, Justin, wrote his *Dialogue with the Rabbi Trypho*, in which the latter says that the Jews also look forward to the Messiah, but as "a man from among men." He accuses Christians of telling stories like the myths of the Greeks; for example, the myth of Perseus who was born of the virginal Danae "after Zeus had descended in the form of gold. You should be ashamed of telling such stories. It would be better for you to assert that this Jesus had been born as a man among men" (*Dialogue*, 99, 67). Sometimes the polemics were even sharper. Even as early as the end of the first century various stories are said to have circulated that changed Jesus' alleged virginal birth into an indiscretion with a Roman soldier on the part of Mary.

The polemics originating from pagan writers tend in the same direction. Celsus, who wrote his attack on Christianity in AD 178, takes up the Jewish polemics and writes ironically about God's love affair with an insignificant Jewish girl. Pagan attacks on this article of faith are mostly at this same level.

In spite of all these attacks, the teaching concerning the Virgin Birth was held fast; this shows that it cannot be explained in terms of what was found plausible at the time. This is even clearer if we take into account the disputes that were going on in the Church. In second-century Gnosticism the Virgin Birth was partly rejected and partly accepted, but in a way that denied the real Incarnation: it was said that the Logos went through Mary as through a channel or tube.

Why did the Church hold on to this belief so tenaciously in the teeth of large-scale mockery and misunderstanding? We may get an idea by comparing that other "eloquent mystery" of which Ignatius of Antioch speaks: the death of Jesus on the Cross. This death is so offensive to *all* mankind, not only to Jews and pagans, but to Christians as well, that it must be based on historical fact; this alone can explain why people try to understand it and interpret it, and even start preaching it. Fact comes before interpretation. Precisely *because* it is so hard to grasp, such a stumbling block, the fact acts as a spur to interpretation. The Cross could never be deduced from Jewish or Hellenistic models. It is the *fact* that Jesus died an accursed death on the Cross of shame that has made it possible to see a meaning in *this* terrible event, a meaning foreshadowed far back in the Old Testament.

Something similar seems to be the case with the Virgin Birth. No one "invents" something that provokes derision and misunderstanding all around! The only sensible interpretation seems to be this: the *fact* of a solid tradition in the primitive Church regarding the conception of Jesus by the power of the Holy Spirit is the *starting-point* of all the attempts to understand, interpret, and actually proclaim this baffling, even repellent fact. Subsequent reflection uncovered the connections with Old Testament prophecies and brought out the inner relationship between Jesus' life and his Spirit-wrought conception.

Does not human experience suggest that this is the likely course of events? At critical moments in our experience it is the facts that come first, events that stamp our lives. Initially, they do not seem to be part of an intelligible whole (e.g., a sudden death, a failure, an unexpected meeting). But gradually the meaning reveals itself; what originally lay across our life's plan as an obstacle can symbolize an entirely new meaning to life. What seems to others, outsiders, to be nothing but a meaningless fragment encountered along life's path, can unfold a deep symbolism for the person concerned. (Here I am thinking of the meaning that emerged in the life of my own family as a result of their having to flee from their homeland.) The fact comes before the disclosure of its meaning; and once the meaning has been disclosed, it becomes possible to see the fact itself in a wider context of meaning. Indeed, it becomes possible to say "it *had* to happen like this; this made more sense." No one, however, will suggest that the subsequent understanding can explain and construct the fact.

If we apply this to the question at issue, it emerges that the Virgin Birth is too unexpected, too alien, to have been constructed in the manner of a theologoumenon. It is the *fact* of the tradition of this mysterious event that causes people to ask about its meaning. Conversely, the context of meaning that was disclosed to the primitive community, as it reflected on what had taken place, actually expanded the field of vision; as a result, this event was seen to correspond explicitly to the "logic" of God's activity.

Before we examine the symbolic content of the doctrine of the Virgin Birth, let me put forward an entirely personal hypothesis on the way this "disclosure of meaning" takes place in history. This is a risk, I know, but surely a time like ours, which produces such a quantity of exegetical hypotheses, is tolerant enough to give a hearing to the perhaps rather naive conviction—simply as a hypothesis—of one who is, exegetically speaking, a layman.

When can we posit the origin of the community's tradition that Jesus was conceived by the Holy Spirit? It seems to me worth considering that the beginnings of this tradition may be associated with the primitive Church's *experience of the Spirit*. Luke clearly describes the Church's "birth" at

Pentecost in parallel with the account of Jesus' birth: in both "cases" it is the descent of the Spirit that effects the miraculous birth. We might be strongly inclined to see this parallelism as a theological "construct"; but might not the reverse be the case? Perhaps it was the original Jerusalem community's *experience of the Spirit* that enabled Christians of the first generation to understand "from within," from their own experience of the Spirit, the significance of Jesus' conception by the Spirit? Let me take my hypothesis further: is it not possible that, for Mary herself, it was the Church's experience of the Spirit which became the "hermeneutical locus"; the experiential milieu within which she became able to speak of the miracle of her conceiving by the Spirit?

Allow me to pursue this line of thought a little: the primitive Church's experience of the Spirit was doubtless that of an event which rendered the meaning of the figure of Jesus transparent and evident. Does it not make sense to assume that this experience of the Spirit, in which Mary shared (Acts 1:14; 2:1), provided the primitive community with that background of experience and understanding that was necessary if it was to properly receive the message of Jesus' conception by the overshadowing of the Spirit?

There is nothing extravagant about such a hypothesis, particularly if we remember that, characteristically, the primitive Church's experience of the Spirit not only opens up an understanding of Christ but also configures believers to Christ. For Paul, the baptized, filled with the Spirit, live "in Christ"; they have died with him and have been raised with him, and now live "hidden with Christ in God" (Col 3:3). John goes one step further: the baptized are also *born* anew, born of the *Spirit* (cf. John 3:5, 8): this birth is "not of blood, nor of the will of the flesh, nor of the will of man, but of God" (John 1:13). "One does not become a child of God by natural birth, not by any natural process of growth, but as a result of a supernatural event worked by God alone" (Schnackenburg, 238). It is only by *new birth* that one can become a new man, a "new creation" (2 Cor 5:17). Very early on, many of the Church Fathers (Justin, Hippolytus, Irenaeus, Tertullian) and many textual witnesses read the passage from the Prologue of the Gospel of John in the singular: "*He* who is conceived not of blood…but of God," and interpret the passage as testimony to the conception of Jesus by the Spirit. This reading is probably secondary, but all the same, it at least shows the primitive Church's profound awareness of a special relationship between the Christian's experience of the Spirit-new birth through the Spirit and the origin of Jesus' life through the operation of the Spirit. Thus, the *reality* of Jesus' conception through the action of the Divine Spirit became the *guarantee* that our "being born of water and the Spirit" (John 3:5) really communicates a *new* life.

History clearly shows us that the second century saw much teaching in defense of the Virgin Birth. But this was not a case of blind apologetics on behalf of some irrational and curious notion. What was at stake was *both* that God had really become man, and that this humanity was really new. All the power manifested in the symbols and images of this new humanity arises from the *reality* of the new beginning wrought by the Spirit.

THE BIBLE'S SYMBOLIC LANGUAGE

In a very stimulating little study, H. Gese has shown how deeply—despite its newness—the theme of the Virgin

Birth is rooted in the Old Testament. Here we can only briefly summarize Gese's results.

In both "infancy narratives" in Luke and Matthew, the birth of Jesus is interpreted as the appearance of the eschatological Scion of David. The promised child "will be great, and will be called the Son of the Most High; and the Lord God will give to him the throne of his father David, and he will reign over the house of Jacob forever; and of his kingdom there will be no end" (Luke 1:32ff.). The promised Scion of David is both "Son of the Most High" and Son of David. This unique "juxtaposition of divine birth and human genealogy" (Gese, 134) is already a trait of Old Testament Davidic kingship theology. The new king ascends the throne accompanied by the singing of Psalm 2, which in the New Testament is applied to Christ: "You are my son, today I have begotten you." Here we have a "unique interplay of divine and human fatherhood" (Gese, 137): for to become King on Zion, where the presence of God "rests" in the Ark of the Covenant, the place of God's presence, which he has chosen (cf. Ps 32), means becoming the "Son of God" in a sense that is entirely realistic. Thus, in Psalm 2:6, the King who is "born today" can say: "I was *created* [in a miraculous way] as his King on Zion, his holy mountain" (cf. Gese, 139).

In the great prophecy of Isaiah with which we are so familiar from the Christmas liturgy, a new Son of David is promised: "To us a child is born, to us a son is given; and the government will be upon his shoulder." It is emphasized even more clearly that this new beginning is "created" by God himself at a time of darkness and defeat: "the zeal of the Lord of hosts will do this" (Isa 9:5ff.). Here, simultaneously, physical birth is seen in close connection with enthronement and divine birth. This becomes highly explicit in the celebrated prophecy to King Ahaz concerning the birth of Immanuel (Isa 7:10–17): the true Son of David promised here ("Behold, a young woman shall conceive and bear a son, and shall call his name Immanuel") is no longer a physical descendant of the "House of David" (v. 13), but a new King whose coming is in secret, and who will be called "God is with us." This amounts to a promise of judgment against the faithless House of David (vv. 17ff.). By contrast, attention is pointed toward the *alma*, that young woman who is to give birth to the new, *true* Son of David. Since the promise was not fulfilled directly, hope was henceforth directed more and more toward an entirely new, final future that would surpass everything known hitherto.

What we have here is an increasing convergence of two lines of prophecy: the promise that God himself will come down as he once did to rescue his people from Egypt—or rather, in an entirely new, magnificent, and definitive way; and the promise that God will raise up a scion for David who will save his people, "and he himself shall be peace" (Mic 5:5).

In retrospect, the primitive Church could see that these two lines ultimately converge in the birth of Jesus. In the subtle symbols and Old Testament parallels of the "infancy narratives" (especially in Luke), it is made clear that the birth of Jesus "is the *whole* gospel" (Gese, 145), the good news of God's coming into this world. Luke interprets Mary on the one hand as "Daughter of Zion" and on the other hand as the "Ark of the Covenant": in this way he shows that she is "the door through whom divine salvation enters this world" (Gese, 143ff.).

We can be fairly certain that the angelic salutation: "*Chaire*—rejoice" (Luke 1:28) involves a reference to the prophecy of Zephaniah 3:14–18: "Sing aloud, O daughter of Zion; shout, O Israel...the King of Israel, the Lord, is in your midst." The angel's greeting announces the great messianic joy. In magnificent typology Mary is seen as the ultimate Zion, the place where God dwells among men: "Do not fear, O Zion...Yahweh, your God, is in your midst [literally: in your womb], a warrior who gives victory" (Zeph 3:16ff.; cf. Luke 1:30ff.; Laurentin, 75–82). Thus, Mary is "the true Zion in person...She *is* the true Israel...She is the 'people of God', bearing fruit by God's gracious power" (Ratzinger, 41).

However, Mary also appears as the typological fulfillment of the Ark of the Covenant. Mary's visit to Elizabeth (Luke 1:39–45) is full of references to David's return of the Ark of the Covenant to Jerusalem (2 Sam 6:2–11): both events take place in the mountains of Judah; both are the cause of great joy (the joy of the people of Jerusalem; the joy of Elizabeth and the child); the child's leaping in Elizabeth's womb corresponds to David's dance of joy; and finally David's exclamation, "How can the Ark of the Lord come to me?" is a parallel with Elizabeth's "And why is this granted me, that the mother of my Lord should come to me?" (2 Sam 6:9; Luke 1:43). So Luke sees Mary as the Ark of the Covenant in whom and through whom God finally makes his abode among his people.

Let us briefly mention one further typology: the symbolism of "God's indwelling" in Mary (as Zion and Ark of the Covenant) is complemented by that of the *Tabernacle* of the Covenant. The conception wrought by the Spirit is proclaimed in Luke in words that clearly recall the cloud of God's glory which descended upon the Tabernacle: "The Holy Spirit will come upon you, and the power of the Most

High will overshadow you; therefore the child to be born will be called holy, the Son of God" (Exod 40:35).

This does not exhaust the wealth of biblical symbolism. The liturgy is the ideal place for such symbolism; there we are continually being introduced to it. Of course this presupposes that people are receptive to symbols, and this is often denied nowadays. We take a different view. It is precisely these powerful and profound symbols of biblical typology that speak to people, now as before, because they touch deep longings and enable them to be expressed. That is why we should have confidence to re-learn the Bible's language of symbols and use it.

He Has Become Man

In this meditation we shall examine two aspects of the topic of Incarnation.

1. Continuing our reflections on the phrase "Born of the Virgin," we ask about the significance of the virginal conception—effected by the Spirit—for our understanding of what is *new* in Christ's humanity.
2. Finally, we go on to look at the ultimate *goal* of the Incarnation.

A LIFE WROUGHT BY THE SPIRIT: THE ROOTS OF THE NEW MAN

The Bible's symbolic language says of the human Child born of Mary that he is himself "God's indwelling" among men. God himself is "Israel's King in your midst" (Zeph 3:14). At the same time, he is a *human child*, completely unspectacular, with a humanity that is beyond all doubt.

Even the prophets were filled with the Spirit, seized by the Spirit, some of them "from the womb" like John the Baptist (Luke 1:15). The Spirit-wrought conception of Jesus says more: it says "this Child's origin is wholly the result of divine action" (Schürmann, 53); he is not only *filled* with the Spirit: God's Spirit determines his innermost being and existence. That is the essential meaning of the doctrine of the Virgin Birth. Let us try, to some degree, to unlock it.

As Old Testament prophecy proceeds, the coming of God is described ever more clearly as a coming that will *make all things new* (cf. Is 43:19). Jesus' preaching, his public activity, his signs, were felt to be astonishingly new (cf. Mark 1:22, 27; 2:12). The primitive Church understood his death and resurrection as the powerful dawning of eschatological renewal (cf. 2 Cor 5:17; Rev 21:1; etc.). But what was this new thing? Is not Ecclesiastes right to be skeptical? "What has been is what will be, and what has been done is what will be done; and there is nothing new under the sun" (Ecc 1:9)? Are not the mockers right when they say that nothing has changed in the world because of Christ's coming? "Where is the promise of his coming? For ever since the fathers fell asleep, all things have continued as they were from the beginning of creation" (2 Pet 3:4).

Here Christ's conception through the Spirit acquires its full range of application: here is *one* man whose existence is entirely new, right from its root. In the midst of a world where anything new simply replaces something old, only to become old in its turn, there is now a *new* humanity, a human life that does not, at its conception, have the germ of death in it, but comes forth entirely out of God's newness.

The Bible knows that no human being is born without being part of a history of guilt. He inherits this guilt and transmits it (as is ruthlessly demonstrated by Jesus' family tree in the Gospel of Matthew): "Behold, I was brought forth in iniquity, and in sin did my mother conceive me" (Ps 51:5). Can we imagine a human existence that is free, from its inception, from implication in guilt? Can we imagine a life that is holy, sinless, right down to its roots? This is precisely what Jesus' conception by the Spirit affirms.

A sinless existence? One often hears it said that to maintain that Jesus was sinless is to compromise his genuine humanity. This view manifests a total misunderstanding of sin. If sin means saying "No" to God, a "No" that also results in a breaking of relationships with one's neighbor, it follows that sin is the germ of death in a very real and concrete sense (cf. Rom 5:12). Sinless existence, by contrast, means being human and open to God and to one's neighbor. Here we discern the whole scope of faith in the Virgin Birth: from Jesus' new *conception* flows his new *life*. His Spirit-wrought existence makes possible a humanity that is unrestrictedly open to God *right down to its roots*, to such an extent that, for him, God is always "Abba," Father. His life, flowing from its origin in the Spirit's activity, is also the deepest ground of that unbelievable openness in his encounters with other human beings. Merely to encounter this man was to be made whole; here was a man who never abandoned the wounded along his path. Being human without wounding others: can we not understand *Spirit-wrought* humanity in this way? Is this not the very opposite of our humanity that is stamped by sin, always wounding others even while it subscribes to the good?

A new man: completely open to the Father, completely open to his brothers. Death, a consequence of sin, has no power over this life. On the other hand it *is* vulnerable: anyone who is open in this way, at the innermost source of his existence, is also "unprotected" against the harshness of evil, of sin. If we are right to see the deepest reason for Jesus' openness in the fact that his existence is a work of the Spirit, it follows that we must see the reason for his *death* here too. *His* path to death was not the natural consequence of his birth as ours is. He walked toward death because his life was not in any way self-centered. Since he was completely open to everyone, the guilt of everyone fell upon him. "Surely he has borne our griefs and carried our sorrows"—so Matthew interprets the openness of Jesus in the light of the Suffering Servant (Isa 53:4; Matt 8:17).

Thus the circle is closed: since he was conceived by the Holy Spirit and born of Mary's unreserved "Yes," his death too is a dying "for us" (1 Cor 15:3); and that is why death could have no power over him (Acts 2:27); right from his conception, death could find no foothold in this new, Spirit-wrought life.

We profess all these mysteries in the Creed: Jesus was conceived by the Spirit and born of the Virgin Mary; he died for us and our salvation; he has risen and now rules in eternity. Often these things seem like an unrelated list of beliefs, but if we are receptive to the *nexus mysteriorum*, the interconnection of mysteries, if we look at the reverse side of the carpet and see the links, we see a picture of great coherence and harmony. It *all* depends on our having the courage to be uncomplicated enough to believe in the reality of these mysteries. Only when we do this will they begin to reveal their radiance.

DIVINIZATION: THE GOAL OF THE NEW MAN

According to the Preface for Christmas, the ultimate goal of the Incarnation is man's "divinization:" "*You have brought about a wondrous exchange; your divine Word became a mortal man, and in Christ we mortal men receive your divine life.*" The theme of the "wondrous exchange" informs the entire Christmas liturgy. Thus the Collect for Christmas says, "*Grant us to share in the divinity of your Son, who has put on our human nature*"; or in the Offertory Prayer for December 29th: "*Lord, we present our gifts to you for that celebration in which a holy exchange takes place. Graciously accept them, and give us yourself in your Son Jesus Christ.*"

Ever since the beginning of Christian theology, the reason given for the Incarnation has always been that "God became man so that man might become God." We find the same topic as late as Angelus Silesius (III, 20):

"Look! God becometh I, comes down to misery
On earth; I enter thus his kingdom and be He."

Some people today vehemently oppose this view of the goal. The psychoanalyst H. E. Richter traces the entire crisis of technological civilization back to a western "God-complex" of epidemic proportions; that is, to the exaggerated desire for godlike omnipotence that wants to control everything and is incapable of suffering, sympathy, and renunciation out of solidarity for others. The philosopher E. Topisch assesses man's various mystical and political ways of "becoming God" and puts the skeptical question: "And what if man were finally to become God? What good would it do him?" The theologian Hans Kung put the question in a more generalized form: "Does any rational man today want to become God?" We can understand this skepticism as a reaction to the dangers unleashed by man's boundless overestimation of himself; it admonishes us to be moderate in our ambitions and to accept the failures and renunciations without which mankind's survival seems more and more threatened. However, the call to resist the longing to be "like God" becomes problematical if the only alternative offered is the abandonment of every "yearning for the 'Wholly Other'" (M. Horkheimer). Contenting ourselves with a transitory existence, the denial of every yearning to transcend the boundaries of finitude and mortality; this cannot be the solution. It is hard to see how this kind of limited ambition could motivate people to practice solidarity with others, to share their sufferings and be ready for sacrifice.

The Christian ideal of man's divinization does not indicate a path of self-divinization: it is in fact man's *healing* from the "God-complex," from the compulsion of wanting to become like God; it is man's *healing* from a view of God that projects the reverse image of his own powerlessness on to a despotic, omnipotent God.

The Christmas theme of the "wondrous exchange" gives the direction in which we should look for the Christian idea of how man can "become God." Paul shows the way: "You know the grace of our Lord Jesus Christ, that though he was rich, yet for your sake he became poor, so that by his poverty you might become rich" (2 Cor 8:9). Thus, the Christian path of divinization can only be a path that makes man like God, like him in his "self-emptying" (Phil 2:7), which makes us rich. The goal of God's Incarnation is man's divinization. And as for the path to this goal, it can be none other than the path taken by the Son of God in becoming man for us.

Gregory of Nyssa once formulated the Pauline theme in this way: "God takes on the poverty of my flesh so that I may receive the riches of his godhead" (PG 35, 325). This exchange, or as Luther calls it, this "joyful converse," is at the center of the Christmas icon that is the subject of the following, concluding meditation. The icon's picture-language meditates on both aspects: how God, becoming man, adopts my poor flesh; and how I receive from his poverty the riches of his divine life.

The Christmas Icon

THE INCARNATION IN THE LANGUAGE OF THE ICONS

Icons and their unique world of images are no longer strange and unfamiliar in our cultural milieu. We know them at least as works of art. The fascination they exert is all the more remarkable when we consider that the meaning of icon "language" is, for the most part, still not understood. Compared with the realistic and often sentimental representations of Christmas in western art, the Christmas icons have a mysterious and solemn effect. Perhaps it is precisely this difference that makes icons attractive. The following interpretations, which touch on art history and draw on the liturgical texts, do not attempt to simply "explain" what the picture means, but rather to let the language of the icons give its own message.

AN ANCIENT PICTORIAL TRADITION

The five Christmas icons in this little book belong to a period of time that embraces at least one thousand years. From the oldest picture (sixth century) to the youngest (sixteenth century), certain basic compositional elements persist, elements that contrast surprisingly with the Western idea of Christmas that has become current since the late Middle Ages. Here Mary and Joseph do not kneel in adoration of the Child: the Child lies neither in a crib nor in a stall. Instead, generally, Mary takes a prominent position in the center of the picture, lying on a cushion-like bed. Her gaze is often turned away from the Child; Joseph most often sits at some distance from Mother and Child, withdrawn and brooding. Finally, the Child lies in a cave on a structure resembling an altar, firmly wrapped up in linen cloths. He is almost always accompanied by the two nursemaids who bathe the Child: Western art hardly ever mentions them; it is more familiar with the angels, the shepherds, and the wise men from the East. Again we find the arrangement in the Eastern Church's pictorial tradition unusual. The astonishing constancy of this tradition is new to us. With our modern notion of art, we are inclined to see this as a sign of rigid traditionalism, of a lack of creativity. We need to be cautious, receptive, and open if we are to overcome such prejudices. This severe adherence to the iconographic model is anything but a blinkered imitation of what has gone before. Rather, the artists are always seeking a new way of uttering the same great mystery. We need to be familiar with icons for a long time before we can see how new and unique each icon is, and how little the artist's freedom is restricted by the existence of a given school of depiction.

The best way to understand the characteristics of this school of painting is to relate it to what the Church taught about the person and mission of Christ, especially in the first great Councils. The Christmas icon is entirely constructed around the mystery of the Incarnation. It is a profession of faith in the true Incarnation of God, not abstractly, in dogmatic formulae, but in the visible language of pictorial expression.

"A GREAT LIGHT…"

The Christmas icon does not represent the historical night of the birth in Bethlehem, but, symbolically, the darkness of the world into which the light of this great hope has exploded. Thus there is a subtle play of light and dark; the dark cave contrasts with the "great light from on high" that, according to the Song of Zachariah, lightens "those who sit in darkness and in the shadow of death" (Luke 1:78ff.). The star in the Christmas icon "distills," as it were, the fullness of light, which comes from above to drench the whole picture. Initially of course the star is the one seen by the wise men from the East (Matt 2:2, 9, 10). Generally the traveling wise men are depicted as pointing to it (icons 3 and 4). At a deeper level it is Christ himself who is this Star. This is how Ambrose of Milan interprets it: "Only the Wise Men can see the Star; where Herod dwells it is invisible, but where Christ dwells it becomes visible and shows the way. So this Star is the way, and Christ is the way, because in the mystery of the Incarnation Christ is the Star. 'For a star shall come forth out of Jacob, and a scepter shall rise out of Israel' (Num 24:17). So wherever Christ is, the Star is also; for He is the 'bright Morning Star' (Rev 22:16). Thus it is with His own light that He points to Himself" (*Commentary on Luke* II, 45).

This light really has shone on earth. So the star is linked with the Child by one or more shafts of light (no. 3): "Above the dark cave there shines the heavenly light; its rays reach the Child, as if to attest that his origin is from this light (Isa 60:1f; Hab 3:4)" (Schiller, 76).

OX AND ASS

We are familiar with these two animals from western depictions of Christmas. They are part of the earliest stratum of the portrayal of Christ's birth. How have these animals found their way into the picture when the evangelists do not mention them? The ox and ass remind us that Christian iconography sets before us many scenes that are not in the four canonical Gospels but come from the kaleidoscopic, and often luxuriant imagination of the Apocrypha. Church leaders and theologians have always campaigned vigorously—and often in vain—against these writings; artists, by contrast, have even managed to secure permanent rights of domicile in the Church for some of these apocryphal stories. Perhaps we should not be too strict here, for the apocryphal gospels are often putting forward a "narrative theology" that is particularly suited to the language of painting.

Thus, we read in the apocryphal "Pseudo-Matthew" (chap. 14): "On the third day after the birth of Our Lord Jesus Christ the most blessed Mary came out of the cave, went into a stall and laid her little boy in a crib, and the ox and the ass worshipped him. Then was fulfilled what the Prophet Isaiah had foretold: 'The ox knows its owner, and the ass its master's crib' (Isa 1:3). In this way even the animals, the ox and the ass, ceaselessly adored him while he was among them. This was to fulfill the words of the Prophet Habakkuk, who said, 'In the midst of two animals you shall be known' (Hab 3:2 LXX)."

It is possible that this fifth century text and the pictorial representation are both rooted in an older tradition in which these prophetic passages were already applied to Christ. More importantly, this picture speaks of what faith professes; namely, that this Child is "the Lord of heaven and earth." Angels, men, and even animals: the whole creation bows in adoration of the Creator who has himself become a creature.

But it does not always have to be a donkey! In Russian icons, the donkey is replaced by a horse (no. 4), perhaps as an expression of the very Russian love of horses. (The horse is a symbol of life; there are magnificent representations of horses in Russian icons.)

"CRIB" AND CAVE

The Evangelist Luke speaks of a "manger" (2:7, 12) where Mary laid her newborn Child. Our icons show a tall walled or stone edifice, like an altar. Is this meant to symbolize the fact that, right from the start, this Child's path leads to the altar of the Cross? In this vein some have spoken of the "altar of the crib" (Drobot, 253) and pointed to the profound connection between Incarnation and Cross; after all, the Gospel of John interprets the Incarnation as the Word becoming bread, "becoming eucharist." A fourth-century pilgrim takes up this theme in saluting the place of Christ's birth: "Hail, Bethlehem, 'House of Bread', where that Bread was born which came down from heaven (cf. John 6:41)" (Nyssen, 83).

This interpretation is supported by the detail that always shows the Child firmly wrapped and bound (no. 3): the parallel to the portrayals of the Laying in the Tomb is striking. As she lays her Child in the crib, Mary as it were performs the sacrificial action of laying him in the tomb. What to us seems like too-daring symbolism is a theme very familiar to the liturgy of the Eastern Church: the rites associated with the preparation of the gifts in the Byzantine liturgy clearly show this relationship. The texts for these rites interpret the preparation of the eucharistic gifts from the perspective of those mysteries in which Christ, in his body, was given up for us: his birth and death (Plank, 156). Finally, there is the cave, which surely also indicates this same relationship. The cave of Christ's tomb, and even the cave of Hades (cf. the Resurrection icon) in which Adam—fallen humanity—lies, is foretold by the cave of his birth: "Glory in the highest to the Triune God, through whom goodwill has appeared among men so that God, the lover of men, may redeem Adam from the primal curse"—as we read in the liturgy of the hours for the Feast of Christmas in the Eastern Church (Onasch, 175–78).

Some may feel that the picture here is too arbitrarily allegorical; but the reverse is the case. This kind of theological typology is characteristic of the language of icons: here we have a translation into the language of painting of what is formulated conceptually by the Creed: "For us and for our salvation he came down from heaven and was made man...." The icon is not interested in the anecdotal, but the typical: the "altar of the crib" and the darkness of the cave of the nativity eloquently set forth the significance of this Child's birth. Right from the beginning of his Incarnation Christ has descended into the depths of that world of death where lies "Adam," i.e., mankind dwelling in the "shadow of death." Could there be a better way of portraying in painting the joy at the birth of Christ than this Child, bathed in light, in the dark mountain cave?

THE MOTHER OF GOD

What often surprises the western observer most of all about the Eastern Church's Christmas icons is that Mary, and not the Child, is at their center; furthermore, Mary usually has her back turned to the Child. However, this has nothing to do with exaggerated Marian veneration; rather, its meaning is to be sought in the pictorial tradition of the Christmas icon itself: whereas the icon of Christ concentrates on the Incarnation of the eternal Word, the Christmas icon is a reflection on the "how" of the Incarnation. The Christmas icon of the Rublyov school (no. 4) is perhaps the most eloquent here. The mother of God (this is the Eastern Church's favorite term for Mary) prominently occupies the center of the picture. Her posture clearly expresses the exhaustion of having given birth; the reality of her motherhood is further emphasized by the placing of her womb at the very center of the picture. In its own way, the icon takes up the words spoken by the woman of the crowd who called to Jesus: "Blessed is the womb that bore you..." (Luke 11:27). Thus, it clearly professes and expresses the real birth, and, hence, the real humanity, of Christ.

At the same time, however, the portrayal of Mary also emphasizes the other side: "In your womb, O Mother of God, you have conceived the Word, the God who has no beginning, who appeared in our nature for our sake, for the sake of mankind," as we read in a Byzantine hymn to Mary (Kirchhoff, 120). Mary's motherhood stands at the center of the icon to express graphically our astonishment that the

Word of God has actually become man. So the iconography stresses both the human motherhood of Mary and her inconceivable dignity; the purple clothing of the mother of God (sometimes it is of royal blue) is a sign of this dignity.

Liturgical parallels indicate that the theme of Mary as mother of God is occasionally given a further symbolic meaning: the mountain and the cave of the nativity are taken to refer to Mary and her maternal womb. Citing Old Testament prophecy (Dan 2:34; Hab 3:3), the Byzantine liturgy sees Mary as the holy mountain whence God proceeds: "Rejoice, Mary, Virgin Mother, Holy Mountain, Eden, Paradise, of whom was born Christ our God" (Onasch, 179). And, even more clearly: "A young child came out of the mountain of the virgin, the word for the new creation of the nations" (Onasch, 182).

These typological and symbolic relationships show that the icons are designed, not to tell a moving story, but to unlock the profound symbols that have become historical reality. History is to become transparent and reveal its deeper meaning.

THE BATH SCENE

This aim is even more evident when the painters seem to be simply recounting anecdotes, as in the two scenes right at the bottom of the picture, on the ground, on the "earth of reality": the Bathing of the Child and the Brooding Joseph.

The bath scene comes from the apocryphal gospels that speak of two nursemaids, even mentioning them by name: Zelomi and Salome. The icon tradition allots them the sole task of bathing the newborn Child; this they do conscientiously, and in most of the depictions one of them tests the bathwater to see if it is at the right temperature!

JOSEPH'S DOUBTS

Whereas the bathing of the Christ-child is designed to show the genuine reality of his human nature, the Joseph scene is concerned with the mystery of the Child's conception through the Holy Spirit and his divine nature. The strange figure in ragged garb who is mostly to be found standing before Joseph is interpreted in different ways: as one of the shepherds, come to worship the Child; as the Prophet Isaiah, who scatters Joseph's doubts and questions by reminding him of the prophecy about the virgin who will conceive (Is 7:14); or as the tempter who plagues Joseph with worrying questions. The Eastern liturgy is not afraid to dramatize Joseph's doubts and Mary's answer in dialogue form. A trope from the Christmas Liturgy of the Hours is the most apt interpretation of the gesture in which Mary addresses Joseph in icon 1:

> "When Joseph, O Virgin,
> was wounded by sorrow
> you spoke to him
> on the way to Bethlehem:
> Why do you grieve
> to see me with child?
> Do you not know the mystery in me
> that causes all to tremble?
> Know then the mystery and henceforward
> be not afraid.
> For by grace

God has come to earth
into my womb
and there taken flesh.
In his good pleasure
you will see him
when he is born
and full of joy
worship him as your Creator
whom the angels ceaselessly
hymn and glorify
together with the Father
and the Holy Ghost." (Jockwig 152)

As we draw these reflections to a close, many a reader may recognize himself most readily in the questionings, doubts, and fears of Joseph; he may feel that, like Joseph, he is sitting on the periphery of the action, brooding, puzzled, and apparently excluded from a story in which he seems to have no place. Let anyone who feels like this be assured that he has understood the language of the icons remarkably well. The questioning figure of Joseph demonstrates something that is typical of icons: the icon does not represent a world that is closed off and that the observer approaches from outside, as a stranger. The picture is open: the onlooker has his own place in the picture; he has a part to play in it and is drawn into the action. It does not intend to represent a past event that is finished and concluded: it wants to draw the observer into an action that is living and present. In the person of Joseph, we are summoned to give up our self-centered brooding and let ourselves be drawn into the mystery that is beyond our comprehension: that God has become man.

Anyone who accepts this invitation will find that the Christmas icon ceases to be simply one work of art among others. In the icon he will encounter the mystery of Christmas itself and be able to say with the Byzantine liturgy:

> "I behold a mystery
> strange and beyond man's grasp:
> the cave becomes heaven,
> the Virgin the cherubim throne,
> the crib the place where He lies
> whom no place can confine:
> Christ, God, whom we
> in song extol."

Bibliography

Barth, K. *Kirchliche Dogmatik*, I, 2. Zurich, 1960.

Brague, R. "Gottes Meisterwerk: Geburt der Kunst aus der christlichen Mitte." *Int. Kath. Zeitschr. Communio* II (1982), 527–44.

Drobot, G., *Icône de la Nativité, Abbaye de Bellefontaine.* 2nd ed., 1975 (Coll. Spiritualité Orientale, no. 15).

Edwards, D. *The Virgin Birth in History and Faith.* London, 1943.

Gamber, K. *Ein kleines Kind—der ewge Gott: Bild und Botschaft von Christi Geburt.* Regensburg, 1980.

Gese, H. "Natus ex Virgine." *Vom Sinai zum Zion.* Munich, 1974.

Goulder, M., ed. *Incarnation and Myth: The Debate Continued.* London, 1979.

Hengel, M. *Der Sohn Gottes.* Tübingen, 1974.

Hick, J., ed. *The Myth of God Incarnate.* London: SCM Press, 1977; Philadelphia: Westminster Press, 1977.

Jockwig, F. "Die liturgischen Texte zur Feier des Weihnachtsfestes im byzantinischen Ritus." *Der christliche Osten* 33 (1978), 148–53.

Kirchhoff, K. *Hymnen der Ostkirche.* 2nd ed. Münster, 1960.

Kranz, G. *C. S. Lewis. Studien zu Leben und Werk*. Bonn, 1974.

Kuhn, P. *Gottes Selbsterniedrigung in der Theologie der Rabbinen*. Munich, 1968.

Laurentin, R. *Struktur und Theologie der lukanischen Kindheitsgeschichte*. Stuttgart, 1967.

Lewis, C. S. *God in the Dock: Essays on Theology and Ethics*. Grand Rapids: Eerdmans Publishing Co., 1970.

Lewis, C. S. *Miracles*. New York: Macmillan, 1947.

Machen, J. G. *The Virgin Birth of Christ*. London, 1930.

Mauser, U. *Gottesbild und Menschwerdung*. Tübingen, 1971.

McHugh, J. *The Mother of Jesus in the New Testament*. London, 1975.

Nyssen, W. *Frühchristliches Byzanz*. 5th ed. Trier, 1978. (Reihe "Sophia" bk. 2).

Onasch, K. *Das Weihnachtsfest im orthodoxen Kirchenjahr: Liturgie und Ikonographie*. Berlin, 1958.

Plank, P. "Die Weihnachtsikone der byzantinischen Orthodoxie." *Der Christliche Osten* 33 (1978), 153–58.

Rahner, H. *Griechische Mythen in christlicher Deutung*. 3rd ed. Zurich, 1966.

Ratzinger, J. *Daughter Zion*. San Francisco: Ignatius Press, 1983.

Rordorf, W. "...Qui natus est de Spiritu sancto et Maria Virgine." *Augustinianum* 20 (1980), 545–57.

Schiller, G. *Ikonographie der christlichen Kunst*. Gütersloh, 1966.

Schnackenburg, R. *Das Johannesevangelium*. I. Freiburg, 1965.

Schürmann, H. *Das Lukasevangelium*. I. Freiburg, 1969.

Solouchin, W. *Schwarze Ikonen. Ich entdecke das verborgene Russland*. Salzburg, 1978.

Vogtle, A. "Offene Fragen zur lukanischen Geburts und Kindheitsgeschichte." *Das Evangelium und die Evangelien*. Düsseldorf, 1971.